MW00903734

ISBN: 9781660189267

And Then . . .

by

Roscoe L. Champion

Poems of remembrance in the order they were written in
the year following the death of his beloved wife Barbara

Also by Roscoe L. Champion

Flakes of Time and Other Poems

Life in the Watermelon Works *

Musings *

Musings, Too *

Fourteen Poems for 2014 *

*Self-Published

Dedicated to

Barbara June Champion
Truly a Winner

Foreword

These 31 poems are presented in the sequence they were written over a period of a year and a day. The first came at 4:31 a.m. on December 30th two days after he lost his wife; the last one was penned on December 30th, one year later. These lines have captured the pathos and anguish, the joyous remembrances, and abiding thankfulness experienced that year. They tell an inspirational story of great love, great loss, and the stalwart passage to a new future.

Table of Contents

But . . .

But . . .   God?
But . . .
"What?"
But, I wasn't finished.
"Finished what?"
 Well, . . cuddling.
"OK."
In the hospital . . .
"Yes."
I wanted him to come into my bed and just hold me.
"Yes."
But it was too small.
"How about when you got home?"
Oh, yes, we cuddled. We cuddled both mornings . . . for a
long time.
"Well?"
But only for two mornings. . . . Then I showed up here. I just
had two days.
"Of what?"
Of cuddling in the morning after I left the hospital . . . Then I
left. . . . I don't remember. It didn't hurt. I just left. I miss
him. It wasn't enough.
"Hmmm. Didn't you have 48 years?"
Yes, but . . .
"What?"
That wasn't enough.
"It was a lifetime, wasn't it?"
Yes, but . . .
"What did you do while cuddling?"
Talked. Held each other.
"Yes?"
Just held each other and talked and loved. Just felt totally
enveloped in love. It was so good.
"Yes."

1

But I wanted more.
"More what?"
Time together. He's still down there.
"He'll be along."
When?
"In time."
In time . . . When?
"My time."
Oh . . . .
"Can you count?"
Count what?
"Your earthly blessings."
Oh, yes. We did, every day, but . . .
"But, what?"
We couldn't count that high; there were too many.
"Too many?"
No, no. Too many to count.
"And that was bad?"
Oh, no. that was good. Very good. It was wonderful!
"So?"
It was an incredibly rich life. We were so privileged to do
so much, to go and see and do, but . . .
"What?"
Well . . .
*"Did you know how many lives you impacted for the
good? To make their lives richer? With your attitude and
encouragement and . . . just your presence?"*
No.
"Your smile brightened so many days, in so many lives."
It did?
"Yes."
Oh.
*"You sang so many beautiful melodies, in so many
different events, throughout your long and fruitful life,
down there."*
I did?
"Oh, yes. Now you are ready to sing here."

But my voice . . .
"It's fine now. No problem."
Really?
"Yes, and you have new melodies to learn and sing here."
I do?
"Yes."
Oh, wonderful!   . . .   But . . .
"What?"
I still long to know the joy of cuddling. It was so
meaningful.
"Yes, I know. That's why I instilled that in all of you."
But . . .
"Don't worry, he'll be along."
When?
"In time."
OK.

12-30-18   4:31 a.m.

Meaning

As the light vanishes with a click,
I begin to stalk that elusive phantom
Called sleep.
In the depth of the following darkness,
I also seek solace.
I reach for a reassuring touch
On the other side of the bed,
But find only empty space.

Although the dreams of before
Were wondrously fulfilled,
The longing gnaws at the heart.
Perhaps that will subside with time.
Ahh, but time ticks so slowly now.
Those fleeting moments of joy
Always pass in such brief instants.
But each one has left
Its cherished sensation ---
Like the touch of a child's stuffed animal,
So soft and warm and cuddleable,
Like the touch of her cheek against mine.
Mmmm. But no more.
Lying, gently grieving in the dark.
Then, finally, comes --- stealthily and silently ---
That blessed nothingness called sleep.

And thereby, we are renewed,
Renewed to rise again and
Stand stalwart another day,
While giving thanks for
The blessings of her life,
So joyously intermingled with mine.
Thus giving meaning to both,
All in the full depth of meaning.

Early January 2019

Little Things

It's the little things that bring her back.
Half asleep, I turn over in bed
And find myself attempting to do it softly,
So as not to awaken her.
But she's not there.
I walk into a room and glance at ---------,
And there in my mind is a memory
Of her.
And in my heart, a gentle tug.
No doubt this goes on in the weeks to come,
And, with time --- and healing ---
Perhaps those little things become
Lovely, reassuring little touchstones
Of the abiding love
That was ours.

How blest was I to have found her,
So that we built a lifetime
Of those tender touches
That filled our lives,
Enough to last
The rest of my lifetime.

As it fades from anguish and twinge
To those little joys of loving remembrance,
I shall revel in them all,
For it was good,
So very good.

January 2019

Thanks

Oh, yes . . . . It was SO good.
It had everything --- almost everything
We could have desired.
We had found – in each other –
The companion, the one who completed us.
The one who listened and loved,
Who shared and consoled,
Who helped make us who we were.
We became one . . . two separate, but one.
We'd like to think that
God smiled and said,
"It was good."
A major part of me is simply missing,
No longer there,
And the hole is unfillable.
One must turn and look back,
And utter thankful praise
Of what was.
A lifetime of joy and togetherness,
Of reveling in each minute and day,
Consciously wringing all there was
From each of those days.
Yes, Thank you, my God, who blesses,
Thank you, for her.

Late January 2019

Cast Adrift

Having been emotionally cast adrift,
I search,
Search for and seek
A new path for me.
To where?
What destination?
No.
What journey? and
What purpose?
Hmmm. Not clear just now.
No chart, but
Have fine compass,
Have guidance,
Great gratitude
For the paths most recently trod
In tandem.

Now, solo steps uncertain, but it's
Time to take them with confidence,
And joy, for each day
And each step
On the paths that offer new chances
To savor
Joy, grief, challenge ---
Life.

February 2019

Today's Mail

Well, look . . .
Good mail today,
Not the usual junk.
Had three letters from close friends:
Encouraging, remembering the long years
Of fruitful friendship.
Heartwarming words that
Touched a soft spot.
Teared up a little . . .
Then, in my mind, I said,
"Think I'll just sit here
And cry a while."
So I did.

But, not for sadness.
It was for the joy of the richness
Of the times we had shared.
Of the fun things we did together
That enriched our lives,
That built the long, strong friendships
We have known,
Reminding me,
Once again,
Of the truly exceptional fullness
Of the life I have been so very lucky
To have lived.
The thankfulness simply welled up
And overflowed.

I may do that again
Another day.

March 2019

8

Ninety-Four Nights

Ninety-four nights
Without you.
Each one grieving and lonely,
After tens of thousands together.
That were warm and meaningful,
In touch and in heart.
It was --- and yet,
Is.

For such love is not evanescent,
It lingers,
It delicately hovers,
It pervades,
And leaves a tender touch
To comfort and soothe.

For love
Abides.

4-1-19

Tea and Tears

I sat down with a cup of tea, just to read a while and take time to let my frustrated mind settle down a bit. The challenges of divesting Barbara's things is daunting. The clothes, the lovely scarves, the jewelry – were just HER. It is tough to part with them. They mean so much to me that it is so hard to just give them to Goodwill where they cannot be appreciated for what they meant to us. That kind of feeling is simply not transferrable. There was the joy in Sedona in being together and basking in the setting and browsing through the tantalizing shops. Not really seeking anything in particular, but open to the beauty of what talent and careful hands had created. The entire array of things on display was stimulating. And there, in that almost overlooked tray under a glass-top counter was this piece that looked up at us and quietly declared, "I'm supposed to go around Barbara's neck. Tell the store owner that you are to take me home with you." What else could we do?

So many items are like that. We so enjoyed the time together when we found these things. One cannot simply discard them without a thought. The associated memories are too vivid. What to do?

The kids have been offered their choices of what they would like to have. All of those selections went with our blessing. Each recipient admired and wanted it for what it was (a lovely piece of jewelry or a scarf or a blouse, etc.) and its connection to Barbara, but they had no idea of the joyful memories that clung to it. Again, what to do?

I so want them to be valued, appreciated and cherished. Perhaps that is wanting too much. Memories are such intangibles; they exist only in my mind and heart. I guess those cannot be transferred. Thus, I must be content with holding them close to my heart and letting the physical object go its own way to bring memories to someone else. It is only a "thing," isn't it?

In some cases, I have made selections of my own, i.e., chosen a particular piece to go to a certain child or grandchild, or person. In those cases, I have made a quiet presentation of the item to that individual along with the story of where and how and why we acquired it, perhaps sub-consciously hoping they would acquire some of the joy of its inception. Those occasions are relatively few and have been truly appreciated.

There are a few items, treasured by both of us for various memory-laced reasons, that I have not been able to part with yet. Perhaps, after time.

What originally triggered when I sat down to savor my cup of tea and steal away mentally to read an article that I had selected as "contenting" was a story by a lady editor of a small inspirational booklet. She wrote of the meaning of her time with a cup of tea and her father, whose mind had gone on to Never-Never Land and left his physical presence behind. There was a loving pathos between each of the lines printed on the page.

Her words came home to me and brought to mind my personal grief regarding a number of close friends proceeding into that same Never-Never Land. I count several truly close lifelong friends who have embarked on that one-way downhill path.

One cannot help but grieve for that immeasurable loss. The one on the path is oblivious, but each one who loved him or her lives with anguish each and every day. It hurts to watch a vibrant person decline and no longer be who they once were. I guess we can take solace in the blessing that they are truly unaware of their path.

In this extended period of attempting to cope with my intense personal grief at this, the most significant loss of my life, I find myself extremely vulnerable to other's losses. My feelings are very close to the surface and they find easy paths for emotion to break through with anguish and tears. It hurts to hurt, but I do.

As I sat and contemplated in this time of introspection, emotion and tears, my mind groped for --- for what? Solace? Maybe. Inspiration? Perhaps. Understanding? Hmmm. What? Then there came words from Paul's letter to the Corinthians, the noted part about Love: in particular it was the phrase, "love endureth all things."

For I loved these friends, these close personal friends, and I guess it is a form of God's love that I grieve for those, like me, suffering the loss of a spouse in one way or another. Lord knows that there is plenty of suffering here all across this old world.

So I just sat and cried. And wrote. And cried and cried some more. Eventually . . . eventually life goes on. There are many alternatives to choose from in that "going on." So I make my choice; it is with such great thankfulness for the life experiences I have had, for the love I have known with Barbara, and with a joyful outlook for each new day as it dawns.

Life is good.

4-29-19

It's Finally Spring

She died in mid-winter
. . . just three days after Christmas.

Now it's Spring,
And all the flowers are in bloom,
The roses that she loved.
There's a new Peace rose
Glistening in our flower bed.
The one that inspired
A line in a poem,
"I'll never see a rose called Peace,
But what I think of thee."

As everything now blooms to share
Their delicacy, beauty and fragrance,
I can no longer call to her and say,
"O, come and look . . . "
Cannot cut a rose and bring it to her.

Yet, I have these precious memories
Of doing just that, time and again,
Of sharing so much more
For so many Springs,
For so many moments
Together.

As sure as roses continue to bloom,
I will return to our memories' bounteous garden
And select a few lovely roses,
Bring them in,
Set them in a familiar vase
To share them --- even now --- with her.

And find
Peace.

Early May

Cry?

Oh, yes. I cry.
So much easier now,
And more often.
I cry as I remember little things,
Little touches of life
That meant much then, and mean much now.

I cry at a touching story, read or watched.
I cry at the inspiration of a teacher
Which lasts the lifetime of a student
Who comes to know the importance of that gift.
I cry as much in happiness as I do in sorrow.
I cry as I watch another choke up
And find it impossible for their voice
Not to go uncontrollably squeaky and halting.
I cry right along with them in heartfelt empathy.
My emotions are very close to the surface,
And it doesn't take much to let them rise to full bloom,
As tears well in my eyes, and spill over down my cheek.
I know the hurt. I have tasted the same draft,
As the joys and the sorrows of life get easily intermingled.
It hurts; and yet it heals.

5-8-19

One More Blessing

I'm grateful, Lord,
She did not go through
That slow, agonizing path to oblivion.
She was so alert, so thoughtful and caring,
So enthusiastic and
Bright and ALIVE!
Each day,
Even all of that fatal morning,
Until the unexpected end.

Just one more blessing to count,
For she remained, always, who she was ---
Great heart,
Great smile,
All the way.

5-18-19

Do You Remember . . . ?

One of the innumerable joys
Of a long, happy, exciting marriage
Is the unexpected moment when
One's fleeting thought is spoken,
"Do you remember . . . ?"
And an olden incident is recalled.

With the following pause,
Eyes meet, hands touch, smiles break out, and
A familiar tender hug
Speaks volumes in the silence of the embrace.
The remembered incident of one small moment
Of life together, a happening
That sparked into memory a magic moment
That tucked itself firmly into their bank
Of meaningful togetherness.

As they relax the hold of the enfolding arms,
And step apart, the daily routine resumes,
But refreshed by a tender moment that re-asserted
The strong hold of love
Between these two long-joined lives.

Thus life was just made special once again
With the simplest of questions,
"Do you remember . . . ?"

5-22-19

Lovely Full Blossom

It was always there,
This joyous person down deep inside.
It just took time -- and love
To let it all come to the surface
So all could see, enjoy,
And bask in its presence.

It?
Oh, the innate beauty of a unique person.
It doesn't always happen.
But it certainly did with her.
Wondrously so.

When we first met there was a glimpse
Of what welled inside, awaiting nurture.
She was a modestly attractive young woman,
But with sparkling blue eyes and an exceptional smile.
The attraction began early.

The inward beauty was masked
By foregoing experiences of her life.
They had not been the best. Times had been tough,
And it showed, if one would see.
Ah, but more – much more – was about to shine through.

Somehow - - - somehow, we sensed the promise.
There was an unconscious awareness
Of a deeper need, in both,
That the daily contact, the idle conversations
Began to confirm.
And time ticked inexorably by,
Allowing a vision to begin to flicker into possibility.

Over time, and obstacles, the future together
Became necessity, And we followed its mandate.
Through a tortuous path, we came together
With the love between man and woman as God intended.

The bud that was always there in her
Opened into lovely full blossom
Of personhood, of womanhood, of fulfillment.

Photos through those passing years
Clearly show her transition to
The truly lovely, loving, caring, outgoing person
She was meant to be from the beginning.

Abiding, fulfilling love and daily joy, and
The endless blessings of
Year after year of life together
Brought forth in full measure
All that was always there.

Time has chronicled
The bright eyes, the glorious smile
And the beaming countenance
Of who she became and who she was:
A truly beautiful woman.

She lived life fully, and it simply radiated
From her being.
Love, and the freedom it bestowed,
Brought her to crowning fruition.
What cherished memories there are of one
Who became all she was destined to be.
Thankfully, she was mine,
To love and to share.

5-27-19

"Oh, Look!"

"Oh, Look!"
I think, as I drive and see
A gorgeous bush in full bloom
In a neighborhood yard.

Oh, . . .
But there is no one with me.

"Listen to this!"
As I read the paper and find
An interesting fact or story
That I want to share.

Oh, . . .
But that caring, interested companion
Is no longer here.

Time and again,
I find something fascinating,
Something so lovely
Or interesting, or meaningful
That really asks to be shared
With someone else,
With someone attuned to you
Who would respond
With true enjoyment
Of what you shared,
And that you shared.
Sharing thoughts and ideas -- even minutia --
In the many aspects of life
Is part of the pleasure,
Is part of the meaning
Of one's life,
As it twines souls together
In mutual sacrament.

Sharing glances, smiles and dreams,
And all the little things
Of daily life
That make life richer,
That fill lives with joy,
And fill moments
With simple pleasures
Of two who
Care.

Oh, . . .
There's no one there.

6-17-19

It's As If . . .

Late June, soon after her birthday.
The flowers she planted
Have come to full bloom.
The roses are delightfully prolific,
Multiple full blooms and buds
On each and every one.
That one odd plant, the one she nursed
From the beginning and all last year,
Had never bloomed.
This year -- on her birthday --
A dozen large white conical blossoms,
As if in memory of her.
The lawn is greener, the violets abound,
The sage and the lavender are utterly profuse,
And the bees love it.
The lilies are tall and glowing, and
The little glorious hibiscus
Are coming on strong.
Her touch was green in their care,
And they all have responded
As if to say,
"You cared for us,
Just like you did for everyone.
We remember,
Now here is our gift to you.
The only way we can show our love
Is to simply do what we do,
Thrive, bloom, waft our perfume,
Display our colorful petals
To whoever might pass by.
But we know, deep in our roots,
It's for you,
Because you cared."

6-27-19

21

Just Fun

Last night, after the evening news,
As we often did,
I flipped to the "old movies" channel, and
Entered in the middle of a black-and-white oldie.
In that first scene was an old favorite actor,
Never a big star, but a great character actor,
Here an irascible rogue.
The synopsis said the story was about
Twin sisters in love with the same guy.
Two disparate sisters, one being the family black sheep.
Just the thing that would have "hooked" Barbara in 10
seconds.
Once "hooked" she just **had** to continue watching.
I could let it go and go on to bed, but she would protest,
"No, not yet. Maybe at the next commercial --
Or the one after that."
Like a child trying to postpone giving up the day
And going to bed.

I continued watching long enough to see the plot unfold
Until I was ready to head for bed.
As I got up to turn the TV off,
I laughed aloud and spoke to her Presence,
"Barbara Dear, you would have loved this one!"
I hit the Off button on the flinker and
The screen went dark and silent.
I continued to laugh as I headed down the hall.
I said, "Barbara, you rascal, you loved ANY story."
There was such fun in my memories
Of that kind of story playing out again and again.
The fun of little intimate episodes of two people
Living together in love and enjoying all our little quirks.
As I finally turned out the light with
A big smile on my face and in my heart,
I whispered a sweet, "Good night, Barbara."
"I love you."

6-30-19

Once Again

I visited you today,
Again.
So many times since you left.
There was remnant snow scattered here and there
On the first time I was here.
That was the day before the funeral,
When I just had to go see
Where we would be together
Again.

It is such a lovely and peaceful spot.
Seven paces from that large statue
Of Durer's Praying Hands.
I could not have asked for
A more appropriate symbol to be near,
Overlooking the place where
I will finally lie down beside you
Once again, some day.

Often I have taken the time to stop by the cemetery
When I am even somewhat close.
It's easy. It is consoling.
There is an odd finality to standing there
On "my" spot, next to yours,
Seeing our names and the dates of our lives
In burnished bronze, marking
Our lifetime beginnings and ends.
Three of the four dates are there
Awaiting one more for me.

Across the bottom of the marker,
For all to see and understand,
The joy, the story of our lives together:
*"Together we built memories for a lifetime . . . and
beyond"*

On each visit thus far I have been alone.
I speak to you, every time.
Sometimes with a tear,
Sometimes with a laugh aloud
With a flitting thought of a remembered funny incident.
I do not tarry long;
I commune with you
Again.
I have remembered,
I have paid homage to you,
I have missed you, in every possible way.
I have not brought you flowers yet.
But I will, now that there is a receptacle.
Many of my visits are unplanned, but
I'm too near not to stop by
To be comforted
Again.

In coming and going to the car,
I pass perhaps twenty headstones
Each with their story of a life time,
Unknown but to God,
But sandwiched between two simple stark dates.

Each time I find beauty --- and peace.
I see the few scattered trees across
The broad scope of lush green grass.
I see flowers, flags, colorful balloons,
All placed with love and care
In honor of someone they loved.

24

I have seen the season change
From mid-winter to spring and now to summer.
No doubt I will return in the fall
On that singular date in October when we met,
And also when we wed, ten years later.

As I complete my visit and turn to depart,
I gather up the peace of the moment to take with me.
I speak softly to tell you that
I will return,
Again.

7-9-19   4:04 a.m.

Why Do We Cry?

Why do we cry?
We all do,
Probably more often than we'd like.
But why?
I was reading a tender story and
Tears gently welled. They did not spill over,
But certainly blurred my vision.

You know those heartstrings?
Those things stretched tautly
Somewhere between your mind and your heart?
Many things will reach in and pluck a heartstring,
Maybe one you didn't know you had.
They are all coupled to the tears.
Often tears splotch the pages of the book we are reading,
Or the inner pages of a funeral program.

We cry as music so engulfs our being
That we cannot withhold the outpouring.
And the tears and the emotion set us free again.
Free to go on.

I guess we cry because we love.
And, in a way, the tears replenish our souls
So that they may continue to seek
Communion with all we love.

We cry in grief; we cry in joy.
We cry in empathy, we cry in inspiration.
We cry as we set free the emotions that make us human,
Emotions that God placed deeply within each of us
So that our hearts may resonate with our fellow man.

Am I not human?
Do I feel hurt?
Do I see anguish and respond?
How could I not?

Do you feel for others almost as for yourself?
How it hurts down deep inside
When you hold close one who is sobbing uncontrollably?
How could you not?
So the tears -- and love -- are shared.

Perhaps the most touching of all
Are the notes and meaning of "Taps."
Each single note reaches in and grabs the heartstrings
And attempts to tear them loose,
But as each one is released, as if plucked,
They join in a soaring symphony of anguish
That is impossible to quell until
That last haunting note lingers, and slowly fades away.

We cry because we have loved.

8-8-19

Just Joyous

Hey, Kid,
We really did it, didn't we?
Above my desk a dozen pictures
Of places we had to see, together.
Jo Stafford's song from a few decades back:
"Those far-away places with the strange sounding names
Are calling, calling me."
We heard their call --- and answered,
Didn't we?
I lean back in my chair and raise my eyes
To any one of those pictures,
And joyous memories of so many things from each site
Come flooding through my heart.
Remember?   ---
Climbing the steps as high as we could go
On Mont Saint Michel?
Marveling at the totally unexpected links
In the Chain Bridge that connects Buda and Pest?
Thousands of precious memories
That we so delighted in, not just being there
And being together, but Being!
The tranquil peace and glory of sitting on the balcony
Of our hotel room on Santorini,
With a glass of wine, watching the sun set
Over the blue Aegean and the remnant islands
Of one of the world's great cataclysmic events.
Ah, the endless parade of our adventures together.
Just Joyous!
I'm aware of my heart caressing each of the memories
As they are brought back to me throughout each day
By some insignificant thing that reminds me
Of our life together, at somewhere special,
At nowhere special.

Yes, this happens, each day since you've been gone.
How wondrous; how joyously it continues.
How blest I am!

8-9-19

Decision, Question and Answer

A question suddenly flared into my mind.
A question I had not asked myself before.
It comes way into the aftermath of her death.

It happened like this:
Her heart was fluttering, trying to continue to beat.
The paramedics had arrived in response to the call to 911
And had taken over the pumping on her chest.
One asked if we had a DNR.
"Yes."
"May I see it?"
He followed me as I hurried to get it.
Found the book, quickly handed it to him.
I hurried back to the den to be there -- with her.
He found the DNR, checked it and then,
In the most thoughtful way, he said,
"Sir, I know it is tough but you have a decision to make."
And waited.
I stood there absolutely aghast at the decision before me.
My mind raced unbelievably.
Out of all that went through my mind in microseconds,
I remember two stark phrases:
"Heroic efforts" and "To what purpose."
My mind was racing down that path with such velocity
I do not remember much else.

Then those two phrases seemed to meld in my mind,
To allow me to speak the four most reluctant words
I shall ever speak:
"Go with the DNR."

I stood there, steeling myself against the results
That might follow.
I have no idea of the time lapse between my words and
The paramedic's statement as he knelt beside her.
It seemed only a moment until he said quietly,
"Her heart has stopped."

Our life together was over.

In all of these following months
Of grief,
Of healing,
Of remembering,
Of moving on with life,
I have not second guessed my decision.
But, really, it was our decision, together,
Thought about and calmly decided.
The decision had been made, way ahead.
All we had to do was recognize the circumstances
That presented that momentous challenge,
And then invoke the decision.
So I did.

Today, all these months later, as I was reading about
Our individual relationship with our Creator,
I realized that I had never asked Barbara,
"Did I do the right thing?"

And from deep within there came this absolute demand
That this be written, this that you read here.
Through all the tears that flowed as I wrote
I began to feel her response.
I did not sense it; I did not hear it;
I **felt** it.

She was reaching out in reassurance.
Unquestionably, I felt her touch my heart,
And she said, "Yes, my darling,
You had the courage to make that agonizing decision.
It wasn't what we had expected, or wanted,
But you did the right thing. Yes, no regrets.
Once more our love held strong."

8-14-19

Lakeside Dusk

Dusk, and the lake is serene.
A solitary goose smoothly glides across the surface
Leaving a gently expanding V wave behind it.
Near the shore, little circular ripples flare
In multiple places, where small schools
Of black catfish minnows swarm.
The sun, now just below the horizon,
Reaches up under the distant deep gray clouds
And tinges them with that unique
Lovely rose pastel of the arid Southwest.
The dusky golden glow that silhouettes the horizon
Slowly sinks behind it.
The light blue sky follows in its downward arc
With the increasingly dark blue right behind,
Chasing the sun.
A single faint yellow light appears on the far shore
And sends its rippling reflection across the lake.
Suddenly over my shoulder
A flock of thirty or more geese
Swoop low overhead and glide to their landing,
Splashing and stirring the water from its placid calm.
They seek a watery haven as the descending darkness
Says No to further flight.
Their random dots upon the surface fade into the dark.
Above and faintly discerned against the darkening blue
There flits the jerky flights
Of the evening swallows, aerobatically darting
Everywhere in their frenetic feeding ritual,
Chasing their elusive airborne evening meal.
We cannot see how long after dark
They continue to flit and feed.
Evening settles quietly and firmly
As other shore lights send their dancing reflections
In long glittering paths across the now dark lake.
Day is done,
And life is renewing for another God-given day.

8-28-19

Half-Mile from Home

Returning from a week's vacation in a condo
By a lake in Colorado with some of our children,
I turned on the last half-mile toward home,
And, suddenly, it hit home again:
You won't be there.
Empty house . . .
Empty heart for a few blocks.
Had to blink to see good.

One of those unexpected sharp pangs
That catch you unaware.

Missed you on the trip.
Revisited our old haunts in Pagosa.
Kids came up for a few days.
It was a rich time with them.
Just special.
We all thought about you,
Talked about you,
Missed you.
But it was all good, really good.
Yes, as good as it possibly could have been.
Often it was:
"We did this." or "We did that."
"We ate here." or "She fed the stupid geese."

It was all beautiful . . . again.
Rich. Tranquil. Peaceful. Healing.
Miss you.
Thanks for it all.

9-1-19

One Last Time

It was so unexpected.
It was so sudden.
Just after a casual breakfast.
She spoke of nausea, then dizziness.
There wasn't time to say anything,
    To say, "Goodbye."

Now, all these months later,
She came in my dream.
I think she had fallen, but
It was uneventful.
She was not hurt at all.
She calmly asked me to get something for her.
I did, and knelt beside her.
She started to rise, and then,
Grabbed me in a full embrace ---
A total bear hug!
Intense, forceful embrace
With arms squeezing each other tightly.
Our heads were cheek to cheek.
Yet, in the dream,
I could see her face clearly.
Her eyes were wide and bright
With no fear at all ---
Just wide and clear
As we clung to each other.
It was as if she had found a way
To come back,
To come back and hold me one last time.
A time to say, "Goodbye,"
And, "I love you!"
One last time.
And there, in the glory of the embrace,
The dream ended.
She had found a way . . .

10-7-19

Verity

As I finished editing the last poem,
The one about my dream,
I leaned back in my chair and
Looked at the photos above my desk.
Each one held such precious memories
Of our lives together.
As I looked at each one,
I was mentally right there --- with her ---
And it was joyous . . .
    And it hurt.

Emotions welled and tears splotched
The paper on which I wrote.
My gaze went from one photo to another,
To another and another:
Machu Picchu, Mont St. Michel,
The top of Vesuvius, Budapest,
Lahaina Harbor and the great banyan tree,
Tiananmen Square, the Neuschwanstein
Fairytale castle, Santorini, The Duomo in Florence,
The ceiling of the Sistine Chapel.
It had been so rich, so fulfilling,
To have so joyously shared so much.

Hmmm. Once again,
Lives so deeply intertwined in love
Verify that
Love never ends.

10-11-19

October 3, 2019

Our anniversary,
A special date for us.
The day we wed,
The day we met,
Exactly a decade before.
It took a long time,
But the time thereafter
Was worth it,
Worth every joyous thrill of anticipation, and
Every moment of anguish
In dealing with the mountain
That lay ahead of us.

I kind of ignored this day,
This time.
It wasn't so special
Without her.
I can't remember any one
Of those 48 anniversary dates
That we weren't together.
(Even the one at Indian Gardens,
Halfway to the bottom of the Grand Canyon
In the rain.)
I did not allow myself to celebrate
This time.
Her leaving was still too near.
The day just went by, essentially unobserved.

Yet, each day is still so special,
Because of the 17,600 days we had
Together.

That first Third of October day
Was a wondrous beginning,
Of . . . of what?
Of Life! Of Living!

Of making each and every day special,
Filled with love and sharing ---
All those little endearing touches
And glances that speak that most important
Three word phrase,
"I love you."

Yes, we quarreled and got peeved,
All of those little stumbles
That we all do.
Then we let love
Fade them away.
It was life, rich with meaning.

No, I didn't do anything special
To celebrate this particular anniversary,
Nothing more than I do
Each and every day,
For we had truly celebrated life
Together.

11-7-19

And Then . . .

Sometimes,
In the early moments of semi-wakefulness
I think to reach over
And touch her.
And then . . .
"Oh."
"She's not there."

There have been lots
Of moments like that
Throughout the early mornings
Of these long months.
Mostly now, they pass quickly.
Earlier, there was a twinge of heart
As I responded with disappointment,
And a grudging acceptance.
A poignant wish to
Reach out and touch her.

I have to settle for a memory ----
Thousands of memories
Of just such moments
To begin our days,
Renewing the tender bond
Of touch.
For it says so much.

Sometimes,
I reach over through the covers
In a symbolic act of remembrance
Of the utter necessity
Of touching the one you love,
Conveying all you feel
With just a touch.

And then . . .
Life goes on,
Vastly enriched by
All that went before.

11-23-19

Awakening Reverie

I awoke this morning,
My left cheek against my pillow.
Without moving at all,
I opened my eyes.
There on your dresser,
Straight before my gaze,
Was the last formal photo
Of you and me,
Taken only a few months before.
In it were a gray-headed old man,
And a lovely little old lady.
I smiled, broadly, at the two of us.
For, in my mind and in my heart,
You are forever young.
Just as you were when we met,
When we fell in love,
And when we married ---
And all the decades since then.
Young and bright and joyful.
I could feel my cheek against yours,
Smooth and so soft.
I gathered you in my arms
And you were so warm and soft, and tender.
I saw your smile -- that always-welcoming smile
That was so YOU,
The smile so well-remembered by all.
Then I laid there with closed eyes
Just reveling in . . YOU.
You, forever young,
Forever loved.

11-26-19

O-Dark-Forty

Awakened again at O-Dark-Forty.
It seems to be a witching hour for me.
With full consciousness
I cannot find the reins to guide or even slow
My runaway mind.
Random things, old remembrances,
Just myriads of thoughts
Thunder by at full gallop.
Then, on an oval racetrack,
They keep coming back around
Again and again.
Strange things, fun times,
Weird imaginings surface
From the depths of memory.

From the searching heart
Comes a grief counselor's words
On the stages of life after great loss:
Shock, numbness. . . .
Yes, been there, done that.
And after the whirlpool of activities
Necessary to accomplish that which must be done,
There comes this overwhelming darkness ---
Sobs, aches and tears eventually wash grief away.
Next, the grudging acceptance that,
Yes, it's real,
It is not going away.
She really is gone.

As with any great wound,
Eventually scars do form
And cover the raw emotions.
It just takes time --- and patience.
With patience or not, time does pass.

Finally, with that course of time,
Glimmers of a new beginning
Begin to flicker into future possibility.
Thus, the painful passage through the stages
Reaches a solemn resolve, and
A dawn of a new future begins to break.
There is light, there is future,
There is newness of life in that new light.

In so many of the ever-changing stages of life,
New beginnings offer hope,
Offer new challenges and experiences
IF --- IF one will accept them.
Time will inexorably pass,
No matter what I think or feel.
The new beginnings are there
Whether I embrace them or not.
There are choices,
Good and bad, Yes or No.

As my being looks in the mirror
And sees true self,
There comes only one clear choice:
To embrace all that a bright future offers.
Yes, a new future,
Solidly based on the joys of what has been,
While seeking what can be.
The glory of the past neither changes nor fades.
The utter anguish of the loss heals.
What can be is beckoning.

Relentless and eternal time continues its march,
Blessedly allowing me to step forward confidently
Into each new day.
Once again,
I give grateful thanks.

12-12-19

Yesterday, Today and Four Tomorrows

Today, the first few hours of Christmas Eve,
In the midst of the anniversary of
Those fateful, fatal six days
Of a mere year ago,
The first two of those days
Were filled with wrenching
Dread, worry and hope,
For I could do so little for her care.
It was out of my hands.
All I could do was pour all that was me
On to her, all of the love that I possessed,
And, continually, minute by minute,
Keep asking for Divine Help.

As this day dawns,
I do not know how I am.
I thought I was stolid,
Thought I could weather the waves
Of stark remembrance.
As the Four Tomorrows loom,
I am OK,
For I can reach the touchstone
Of the love that we shared,
And find solace.

As these days pass,
As did those of a year ago,
I shall emerge, not unscathed,
But enriched by all that went before,

Time and again in this past year
I have re-lived those six days,
Searching for what I might have done.
I have found no different answers.
I find no regrets, no "what if's . . "
I did all I could.
It was in God's hands.

44

In each of these now-ensuing days,
I am finding acceptance,
Aware that loss, great loss, may be part of life.
As the tomorrows of Tomorrow keep coming,
And they step into my Todays,
I will welcome them with faith and an open heart,
And endless thankfulness.

12-24-19   4:41 am

A Year Ago Today, December 28

It was a year ago today
That she left.
A year of . . .
What?
Grief? . . . Yes.
Of healing? . . . Yes.
Of growth and resilience,
Of thankfulness,
Of joyful rejoicing in the memories
Of all that we had shared.
For it was Good,
So wondrously Good!

Time and again I would speak to her,
"Hey, Kid, we almost did it all!"
Yes, we really did.
The solace comes from the thoughts
Of the joy we had shared,
Of all we got to see and do,
Of all the lives we touched,
Living in love, and
Giving to others.

Her beaming smile touched,
Enlivened, encouraged, blessed so many,
But especially me.

Old adages remain forever true:
"Time heals all things."
But two others have held me steadfast:
"Don't grieve because it's over,
Rejoice because it happened."
The other came in the simplest,
Most meaningful sympathy card of all:

"We do not grieve without first loving;
We do not love without gaining
More than we could ever lose."

At the end of each of the days of this year,
I have ended that day
Tucked cozily in our bed.
Turning out the light, and there in the dark,
Speaking to my Creator,
I say aloud,
"Good evening, God,
This has been a good day."
Then I would tell Him about my day
And all that was good therein.

Yes, this particular date will be forever memorable,
A day of immeasurable anguish.
Yet, as would be my wish
Had I gone first,
That she find solace,
And then find joy
In each and every day thereafter,
Celebrating all the days
That we lived and loved
Together.

12-28-19

Beyond

Now, a year and beyond . . .

Time,
    love,
        faith,
            hope,
                support,
        and
the sharing of grief
Beget healing.
Life goes on.
The future is there,
And it beckons.
I will stride forth into it
With joy in my heart,
And the contentment of having richly known
"The greatest of these is love."

As it is emblazoned on the single bronze marker
At the grave site for the two of us:
***"Together we built memories for a lifetime . . .
and beyond."***

December 30, 2019

Made in the USA
Las Vegas, NV
05 September 2021

29648407R00037